This Guinea pig Care Jour

SYLVIET

Belongs to

Holly. Moulsdale

and my Guinea pig

lilo

About My Guinea pig

Name: ~~My~~ Sylvie

Breed: _____

DOB: _____

Colour: Cream and white

Special Markings _____

_____

My Pledge to My Guinea pig

I promise to

- give my guinea pig fresh food and water every day ✓
- clean my guinea pig's food bowl every day ✓
- change my guinea pig's bedding when it is dirty ✓
- play with my guinea pig every day ✓
- clean my guinea pig's cage every week ✓
- check my guinea pig's health ✓
- take my guinea pig to the vet when it is unwell ✓
- love and care for my guinea pig ✓

Week Starting _____

Daily Tasks	Mon	Tue	Wed	Thu	Fri	Sat	Sun	
Clean Water	✓	✓	✓	✓	✓	✓	✓	
Fresh Food	✓	✓	✓	✓	✓	✓	✓	
Clean Bowls	✓	✓	✓	✓	✓	✓	✓	
Playtime	✓	✓	✓	✓	✓	✓	✓	
Health Check								
Eyes	✓							
Ears								
Teeth								
Claws								

Weekly Checklist

Clean Cage ☐

Change Bedding ☐

Weight _____

Size _____

Food Eaten

Vitamins Given

Week Starting _____

Daily Tasks	Mon	Tue	Wed	Thu	Fri	Sat	Sun	
Clean Water								
Fresh Food								
Clean Bowls								
Playtime								
Health Check								
Eyes								
Ears								
Teeth								
Claws								

Weekly Checklist

Clean Cage ☐

Change Bedding ☐

Weight _____

Size _____

Food Eaten

Vitamins Given

Week Starting _____

Daily Tasks	Mon	Tue	Wed	Thu	Fri	Sat	Sun	
Clean Water								
Fresh Food								
Clean Bowls								
Playtime								
Health Check								
Eyes								
Ears								
Teeth								
Claws								

Weekly Checklist

Clean Cage ☐

Change Bedding ☐

Weight _____

Size _____

Food Eaten

Vitamins Given

Week Starting _____

Daily Tasks	Mon	Tue	Wed	Thu	Fri	Sat	Sun	
Clean Water								
Fresh Food								
Clean Bowls								
Playtime								
Health Check								
Eyes								
Ears								
Teeth								
Claws								

Weekly Checklist

Clean Cage ☐

Change Bedding ☐

Weight ⬜

Size ⬜

Food Eaten

Vitamins Given

Week Starting _____

Daily Tasks	Mon	Tue	Wed	Thu	Fri	Sat	Sun	
Clean Water								
Fresh Food								
Clean Bowls								
Playtime								
Health Check								
Eyes								
Ears								
Teeth								
Claws								

Weekly Checklist

Clean Cage ☐

Change Bedding ☐

Weight _____

Size _____

Food Eaten

Vitamins Given

Week Starting _____

Daily Tasks	Mon	Tue	Wed	Thu	Fri	Sat	Sun	
Clean Water								
Fresh Food								
Clean Bowls								
Playtime								
Health Check								
Eyes								
Ears								
Teeth								
Claws								

Weekly Checklist

Clean Cage ☐

Change Bedding ☐

Weight _____

Size _____

Food Eaten

Vitamins Given

Week Starting _____

Daily Tasks	Mon	Tue	Wed	Thu	Fri	Sat	Sun	
Clean Water								
Fresh Food								
Clean Bowls								
Playtime								
Health Check								
Eyes								
Ears								
Teeth								
Claws								

Weekly Checklist

Clean Cage ☐

Change Bedding ☐

Weight _____

Size _____

Food Eaten

Vitamins Given

Week Starting _____

Daily Tasks	Mon	Tue	Wed	Thu	Fri	Sat	Sun	
Clean Water								
Fresh Food								
Clean Bowls								
Playtime								
Health Check								
Eyes								
Ears								
Teeth								
Claws								

Weekly Checklist

Clean Cage ☐

Change Bedding ☐

Weight _____

Size _____

Food Eaten

Vitamins Given

Week Starting _____

Daily Tasks	Mon	Tue	Wed	Thu	Fri	Sat	Sun	
Clean Water								
Fresh Food								
Clean Bowls								
Playtime								
Health Check								
Eyes								
Ears								
Teeth								
Claws								

Weekly Checklist

Clean Cage ☐

Change Bedding ☐

Weight [   ]

Size [   ]

Food Eaten

Vitamins Given

Week Starting _____

Daily Tasks	Mon	Tue	Wed	Thu	Fri	Sat	Sun	
Clean Water								
Fresh Food								
Clean Bowls								
Playtime								
Health Check								
Eyes								
Ears								
Teeth								
Claws								

Weekly Checklist

Clean Cage ☐

Change Bedding ☐

Weight _____

Size _____

Food Eaten

Vitamins Given

Week Starting _____

Daily Tasks	Mon	Tue	Wed	Thu	Fri	Sat	Sun	
Clean Water								
Fresh Food								
Clean Bowls								
Playtime								
Health Check								
Eyes								
Ears								
Teeth								
Claws								

Weekly Checklist

Clean Cage ☐

Change Bedding ☐

Weight _____

Size _____

Food Eaten

Vitamins Given

Week Starting _____

Daily Tasks	Mon	Tue	Wed	Thu	Fri	Sat	Sun	
Clean Water								
Fresh Food								
Clean Bowls								
Playtime								
Health Check								
Eyes								
Ears								
Teeth								
Claws								

Weekly Checklist

Clean Cage ☐

Change Bedding ☐

Weight ☐

Size ☐

Food Eaten

Vitamins Given

Week Starting _____

Daily Tasks	Mon	Tue	Wed	Thu	Fri	Sat	Sun	
Clean Water								
Fresh Food								
Clean Bowls								
Playtime								
Health Check								
Eyes								
Ears								
Teeth								
Claws								

Weekly Checklist

Clean Cage ☐

Change Bedding ☐

Weight [_____]

Size [_____]

Food Eaten

Vitamins Given

Week Starting _____

Daily Tasks	Mon	Tue	Wed	Thu	Fri	Sat	Sun	
Clean Water								
Fresh Food								
Clean Bowls								
Playtime								
Health Check								
Eyes								
Ears								
Teeth								
Claws								

Weekly Checklist

Clean Cage ☐

Change Bedding ☐

Weight [_____]

Size [_____]

Food Eaten

Vitamins Given

Week Starting _____

Daily Tasks	Mon	Tue	Wed	Thu	Fri	Sat	Sun	
Clean Water								
Fresh Food								
Clean Bowls								
Playtime								
Health Check								
Eyes								
Ears								
Teeth								
Claws								

Weekly Checklist

Clean Cage ☐

Change Bedding ☐

Weight _____

Size _____

Food Eaten

Vitamins Given

Week Starting _____

Daily Tasks	Mon	Tue	Wed	Thu	Fri	Sat	Sun	
Clean Water								
Fresh Food								
Clean Bowls								
Playtime								
Health Check								
Eyes								
Ears								
Teeth								
Claws								

Weekly Checklist

Clean Cage ☐　　**Change Bedding** ☐

Weight _____　　**Size** _____

Food Eaten

Vitamins Given

Week Starting _____

Daily Tasks	Mon	Tue	Wed	Thu	Fri	Sat	Sun	
Clean Water								
Fresh Food								
Clean Bowls								
Playtime								
Health Check								
Eyes								
Ears								
Teeth								
Claws								

Weekly Checklist

Clean Cage ☐

Change Bedding ☐

Weight _____

Size _____

Food Eaten

Vitamins Given

Week Starting _____

Daily Tasks	Mon	Tue	Wed	Thu	Fri	Sat	Sun	
Clean Water								
Fresh Food								
Clean Bowls								
Playtime								
Health Check								
Eyes								
Ears								
Teeth								
Claws								

Weekly Checklist

Clean Cage ☐

Change Bedding ☐

Weight [_____]

Size [_____]

Food Eaten

Vitamins Given

Week Starting _____

Daily Tasks	Mon	Tue	Wed	Thu	Fri	Sat	Sun	
Clean Water								
Fresh Food								
Clean Bowls								
Playtime								
Health Check								
Eyes								
Ears								
Teeth								
Claws								

Weekly Checklist

Clean Cage ☐

Change Bedding ☐

Weight _____

Size _____

Food Eaten

Vitamins Given

Week Starting _____

Daily Tasks	Mon	Tue	Wed	Thu	Fri	Sat	Sun	
Clean Water								
Fresh Food								
Clean Bowls								
Playtime								
Health Check								
Eyes								
Ears								
Teeth								
Claws								

Weekly Checklist

Clean Cage ☐

Change Bedding ☐

Weight _____

Size _____

Food Eaten

Vitamins Given

Week Starting _____

Daily Tasks	Mon	Tue	Wed	Thu	Fri	Sat	Sun	
Clean Water								
Fresh Food								
Clean Bowls								
Playtime								
Health Check								
Eyes								
Ears								
Teeth								
Claws								

Weekly Checklist

Clean Cage ☐   **Change Bedding** ☐

Weight _____   **Size** _____

Food Eaten

Vitamins Given

Week Starting _____

Daily Tasks	Mon	Tue	Wed	Thu	Fri	Sat	Sun	
Clean Water								
Fresh Food								
Clean Bowls								
Playtime								
Health Check								
Eyes								
Ears								
Teeth								
Claws								

Weekly Checklist

Clean Cage ☐

Change Bedding ☐

Weight _____

Size _____

Food Eaten

Vitamins Given

Week Starting _____

Daily Tasks	Mon	Tue	Wed	Thu	Fri	Sat	Sun	
Clean Water								
Fresh Food								
Clean Bowls								
Playtime								
Health Check								
Eyes								
Ears								
Teeth								
Claws								

Weekly Checklist

Clean Cage ☐

Change Bedding ☐

Weight [_____]

Size [_____]

Food Eaten

Vitamins Given

Week Starting _____

Daily Tasks	Mon	Tue	Wed	Thu	Fri	Sat	Sun	
Clean Water								
Fresh Food								
Clean Bowls								
Playtime								
Health Check								
Eyes								
Ears								
Teeth								
Claws								

Weekly Checklist

Clean Cage ☐

Change Bedding ☐

Weight _____

Size _____

Food Eaten

Vitamins Given

Week Starting _____

Daily Tasks	Mon	Tue	Wed	Thu	Fri	Sat	Sun	
Clean Water								
Fresh Food								
Clean Bowls								
Playtime								
Health Check								
Eyes								
Ears								
Teeth								
Claws								

Weekly Checklist

Clean Cage ☐

Change Bedding ☐

Weight [   ]

Size [   ]

Food Eaten

Vitamins Given

Week Starting _____

Daily Tasks	Mon	Tue	Wed	Thu	Fri	Sat	Sun	
Clean Water								
Fresh Food								
Clean Bowls								
Playtime								
Health Check								
Eyes								
Ears								
Teeth								
Claws								

Weekly Checklist

Clean Cage ☐

Change Bedding ☐

Weight _____

Size _____

Food Eaten

Vitamins Given

Week Starting _____

Daily Tasks	Mon	Tue	Wed	Thu	Fri	Sat	Sun	
Clean Water								
Fresh Food								
Clean Bowls								
Playtime								
Health Check								
Eyes								
Ears								
Teeth								
Claws								

Weekly Checklist

Clean Cage ☐ **Change Bedding** ☐

Weight _____ **Size** _____

Food Eaten

Vitamins Given

Week Starting _____

Daily Tasks	Mon	Tue	Wed	Thu	Fri	Sat	Sun	
Clean Water								
Fresh Food								
Clean Bowls								
Playtime								
Health Check								
Eyes								
Ears								
Teeth								
Claws								

Weekly Checklist

Clean Cage ☐   **Change Bedding** ☐

Weight _____   **Size** _____

Food Eaten

Vitamins Given

Week Starting _____

Daily Tasks	Mon	Tue	Wed	Thu	Fri	Sat	Sun	
Clean Water								
Fresh Food								
Clean Bowls								
Playtime								
Health Check								
Eyes								
Ears								
Teeth								
Claws								

Weekly Checklist

Clean Cage ☐

Change Bedding ☐

Weight _____

Size _____

Food Eaten

Vitamins Given

Week Starting _____

Daily Tasks	Mon	Tue	Wed	Thu	Fri	Sat	Sun	
Clean Water								
Fresh Food								
Clean Bowls								
Playtime								
Health Check								
Eyes								
Ears								
Teeth								
Claws								

Weekly Checklist

Clean Cage ☐

Change Bedding ☐

Weight _____

Size _____

Food Eaten

Vitamins Given

Week Starting _____

Daily Tasks	Mon	Tue	Wed	Thu	Fri	Sat	Sun	
Clean Water								
Fresh Food								
Clean Bowls								
Playtime								
Health Check								
Eyes								
Ears								
Teeth								
Claws								

Weekly Checklist

Clean Cage ☐

Change Bedding ☐

Weight [ ]

Size [ ]

Food Eaten

Vitamins Given

Week Starting _____

Daily Tasks	Mon	Tue	Wed	Thu	Fri	Sat	Sun	
Clean Water								
Fresh Food								
Clean Bowls								
Playtime								
Health Check								
Eyes								
Ears								
Teeth								
Claws								

Weekly Checklist

Clean Cage ☐

Change Bedding ☐

Weight _____

Size _____

Food Eaten

Vitamins Given

Week Starting _____

Daily Tasks	Mon	Tue	Wed	Thu	Fri	Sat	Sun	
Clean Water								
Fresh Food								
Clean Bowls								
Playtime								
Health Check								
Eyes								
Ears								
Teeth								
Claws								

Weekly Checklist

Clean Cage ☐

Change Bedding ☐

Weight _____

Size _____

Food Eaten

Vitamins Given

Week Starting _____

Daily Tasks	Mon	Tue	Wed	Thu	Fri	Sat	Sun	
Clean Water								
Fresh Food								
Clean Bowls								
Playtime								
Health Check								
Eyes								
Ears								
Teeth								
Claws								

Weekly Checklist

Clean Cage ☐   **Change Bedding** ☐

Weight [_____]   **Size** [_____]

Food Eaten

Vitamins Given

Week Starting _____

Daily Tasks	Mon	Tue	Wed	Thu	Fri	Sat	Sun	
Clean Water								
Fresh Food								
Clean Bowls								
Playtime								
Health Check								
Eyes								
Ears								
Teeth								
Claws								

Weekly Checklist

Clean Cage ☐

Change Bedding ☐

Weight _____

Size _____

Food Eaten

Vitamins Given

Week Starting _____

Daily Tasks	Mon	Tue	Wed	Thu	Fri	Sat	Sun	
Clean Water								
Fresh Food								
Clean Bowls								
Playtime								
Health Check								
Eyes								
Ears								
Teeth								
Claws								

Weekly Checklist

Clean Cage ☐

Change Bedding ☐

Weight _____

Size _____

Food Eaten

Vitamins Given

Week Starting _____

Daily Tasks	Mon	Tue	Wed	Thu	Fri	Sat	Sun	
Clean Water								
Fresh Food								
Clean Bowls								
Playtime								
Health Check								
Eyes								
Ears								
Teeth								
Claws								

Weekly Checklist

Clean Cage ☐

Change Bedding ☐

Weight _____

Size _____

Food Eaten

Vitamins Given

Week Starting _____

Daily Tasks	Mon	Tue	Wed	Thu	Fri	Sat	Sun	
Clean Water								
Fresh Food								
Clean Bowls								
Playtime								
Health Check								
Eyes								
Ears								
Teeth								
Claws								

Weekly Checklist

Clean Cage ☐

Change Bedding ☐

Weight [_____]

Size [_____]

Food Eaten

Vitamins Given

Week Starting _____

Daily Tasks	Mon	Tue	Wed	Thu	Fri	Sat	Sun	
Clean Water								
Fresh Food								
Clean Bowls								
Playtime								
Health Check								
Eyes								
Ears								
Teeth								
Claws								

Weekly Checklist

Clean Cage ☐

Change Bedding ☐

Weight _____

Size _____

Food Eaten

Vitamins Given

Week Starting _____

Daily Tasks	Mon	Tue	Wed	Thu	Fri	Sat	Sun	
Clean Water								
Fresh Food								
Clean Bowls								
Playtime								
Health Check								
Eyes								
Ears								
Teeth								
Claws								

Weekly Checklist

Clean Cage ☐

Change Bedding ☐

Weight [   ]

Size [   ]

Food Eaten

Vitamins Given

Week Starting _____

Daily Tasks	Mon	Tue	Wed	Thu	Fri	Sat	Sun	
Clean Water								
Fresh Food								
Clean Bowls								
Playtime								
Health Check								
Eyes								
Ears								
Teeth								
Claws								

Weekly Checklist

Clean Cage ☐

Change Bedding ☐

Weight _____

Size _____

Food Eaten

Vitamins Given

Week Starting _____

Daily Tasks	Mon	Tue	Wed	Thu	Fri	Sat	Sun	
Clean Water								
Fresh Food								
Clean Bowls								
Playtime								
Health Check								
Eyes								
Ears								
Teeth								
Claws								

Weekly Checklist

Clean Cage ☐

Change Bedding ☐

Weight _____

Size _____

Food Eaten

Vitamins Given

Week Starting _____

Daily Tasks	Mon	Tue	Wed	Thu	Fri	Sat	Sun	
Clean Water								
Fresh Food								
Clean Bowls								
Playtime								
Health Check								
Eyes								
Ears								
Teeth								
Claws								

Weekly Checklist

Clean Cage ☐

Change Bedding ☐

Weight [_____]

Size [_____]

Food Eaten

Vitamins Given

Week Starting _____

Daily Tasks	Mon	Tue	Wed	Thu	Fri	Sat	Sun	
Clean Water								
Fresh Food								
Clean Bowls								
Playtime								
Health Check								
Eyes								
Ears								
Teeth								
Claws								

Weekly Checklist

Clean Cage ☐

Change Bedding ☐

Weight [_____]

Size [_____]

Food Eaten

Vitamins Given

Week Starting _____

Daily Tasks	Mon	Tue	Wed	Thu	Fri	Sat	Sun	
Clean Water								
Fresh Food								
Clean Bowls								
Playtime								
Health Check								
Eyes								
Ears								
Teeth								
Claws								

Weekly Checklist

Clean Cage ☐

Change Bedding ☐

Weight _____

Size _____

Food Eaten

Vitamins Given

Week Starting _____

Daily Tasks	Mon	Tue	Wed	Thu	Fri	Sat	Sun	
Clean Water								
Fresh Food								
Clean Bowls								
Playtime								
Health Check								
Eyes								
Ears								
Teeth								
Claws								

Weekly Checklist

Clean Cage ☐

Change Bedding ☐

Weight _____

Size _____

Food Eaten

Vitamins Given

Week Starting _____

Daily Tasks	Mon	Tue	Wed	Thu	Fri	Sat	Sun	
Clean Water								
Fresh Food								
Clean Bowls								
Playtime								
Health Check								
Eyes								
Ears								
Teeth								
Claws								

Weekly Checklist

Clean Cage ☐

Change Bedding ☐

Weight

Size

Food Eaten

Vitamins Given

Week Starting _____

Daily Tasks	Mon	Tue	Wed	Thu	Fri	Sat	Sun	
Clean Water								
Fresh Food								
Clean Bowls								
Playtime								
Health Check								
Eyes								
Ears								
Teeth								
Claws								

Weekly Checklist

Clean Cage ☐

Change Bedding ☐

Weight _____

Size _____

Food Eaten

Vitamins Given

Week Starting _____

Daily Tasks	Mon	Tue	Wed	Thu	Fri	Sat	Sun	
Clean Water								
Fresh Food								
Clean Bowls								
Playtime								
Health Check								
Eyes								
Ears								
Teeth								
Claws								

Weekly Checklist

Clean Cage ☐

Change Bedding ☐

Weight _____

Size _____

Food Eaten

Vitamins Given

Week Starting _____

Daily Tasks	Mon	Tue	Wed	Thu	Fri	Sat	Sun	
Clean Water								
Fresh Food								
Clean Bowls								
Playtime								
Health Check								
Eyes								
Ears								
Teeth								
Claws								

Weekly Checklist

Clean Cage ☐   **Change Bedding** ☐

Weight [_____]   **Size** [_____]

Food Eaten

Vitamins Given

Week Starting _____

Daily Tasks	Mon	Tue	Wed	Thu	Fri	Sat	Sun	
Clean Water								
Fresh Food								
Clean Bowls								
Playtime								
Health Check								
Eyes								
Ears								
Teeth								
Claws								

Weekly Checklist

Clean Cage ☐

Change Bedding ☐

Weight _____

Size _____

Food Eaten

Vitamins Given

Week Starting _____

Daily Tasks	Mon	Tue	Wed	Thu	Fri	Sat	Sun	
Clean Water								
Fresh Food								
Clean Bowls								
Playtime								
Health Check								
Eyes								
Ears								
Teeth								
Claws								

Weekly Checklist

Clean Cage ☐

Change Bedding ☐

Weight _____

Size _____

Food Eaten

Vitamins Given

Important Information

Vet Name _____

Vet Number _____

Things I must not feed my guinea pig:

- Chocolate
- Onions
- Garlic
- Mushrooms
- Cabbage
- Bok choy

- Iceberg lettuce
- Avocados
- Nuts
- Potatoes
- Dairy products
- Meat

- Seeds
- Corn kernels
- Peanut butter
- Rhubarb

Notes:

Printed in Great Britain
by Amazon